A Short History
of the
Irish Language

Diarmuid Ó Breasláin
&
Padaí Dwyer

Glór na nGael Bhéal Feirste Thiar

First Published: 1995
Reprinted: January 1996
ISBN 0 9526324 0 3

Copyright ©
Published by
Glór na nGael Bhéal Feirste Thiar
145 Bóthar na bhFál
Béal Feirste BT12 6AF
Supported by the Cultural Traditions Group

Typeset : Barr a' Tí
145 Bóthar na bhFál
Béal Feirste 12

Printed by NOVA Print
Conway St
Belfast 12

Contents

FOREWORD

The Irish language today, both North and South, is experiencing something of a remarkable revival. What is most remarkable is that this revival is not a Government-led initiative primarily, but one based in communities, urban and rural, throughout the country. It is remarkable too in that it is strongly based in areas of high poverty and deprivation where Irish is recognised as a central plank in re-establishing community infrastructure, self-confidence and pride - areas such as Ballymun in Dublin with its flagship bunscoil 'Scoil na tSeachtair Laoch' or Ballymurphy in Belfast where, like Ballymun and a host of other places throughout Ireland, community support for the language initiatives is vital and community support is readily and generously given.

It is probably no coincidence, therefore, that the last holders of the language beacon were also the impoverished and landless, the farmers and people of the Western seaboard who one hundred and fifty years ago this year faced the brunt of the gravest human catastrophe to afflict Ireland, namely the Great Famine, *An Gorta Mór*. Not only was this a human disaster but it proved a final blow to the fortunes of the language in its heartland.

This booklet endeavours to tell the story of the Irish language from its origins, detailing its evolution, literary masterpieces, the Gaelic society that held it in its dominant position for centuries, the attempts at outlawing it and the process by which it found itself being abandoned, particularly in the nineteenth century.

The Revivalist movement is also detailed from early pioneers up to today's initiatives both North and South. Due to the present revival, it now seems certain that there will never be the need to write the last chapter in the history of the Irish language.

We would like to take this opportunity to thank all those who helped in the production of this booklet; in particular the Cultural Traditions Group for funding; John Dallat, Aodán Mac Póilín, Sean Mac Aindreasa, Magaret Mc Nulty for advice and proofing, Kathleen Quinn for the final corrections and Tom Clarke for layout.

Diarmuid Ó Breasláin
Padaí Dwyer

1. The Origins of the Irish Language

Irish stands among modern European languages as one of the oldest in continual use. Whilst the languages of France, Italy, Spain and Britain were being influenced by Latin, due to the expansion of the Roman Empire up to the fifth century, Ireland's isolated position on the western seaboard ensured that external influences were minimal. Certainly Irish has its fair share of loan words coming from Latin and from British Celtic as it was spoken before the Roman and Anglo-Saxon invasions. This was due to trade between the two nations and to the coming of Christianity, with its emphasis on Latin. Henri Hubert, in *The History of the Celtic People*, makes the point that, although numerous journeys were made between the two lands, nowhere is it mentioned that interpreters were necessary. This reflects the similarities between British Celtic as spoken in Britain (the forerunner of modern Welsh) and the Celtic language as spoken in Ireland.

This similarity can be traced back to the Celtic languages as they existed in Europe at the time of the Celtic empire. This was not an empire in the sense of a centrally dominated political unit, but an area with the same language and culture. Unfortunately little linguistic evidence of this period remains, but we know that by 1000 B.C., Celtic had diverged from its original predecessor sufficiently to be considered a separate language.

What, then, was this precursor? Linguistic historians surmise that the forerunner to European languages was a tongue referred to as Indo-European, a language spoken in South Russia and the Near East, in the period 4000 - 3000 B.C. The gradual expansion of these peoples led to the development of separate linguistic groups: Romance - Latin, French and Spanish; Germanic - Norwegian, Dutch, High and Low German; Slavonic - Russian, Yugoslavian and Hungarian. Celtic also emerged as a separate linguistic strand in this period, leading to the development of the modern Celtic languages. These fall into two forms - Q Celts and P Celts. These labels arise from the split in the Celtic groups whilst Britain and Ireland were being settled from Europe. Britain was colonised directly from the Gallo-Belgic region (modern France and Belgium), whilst Ireland was colonised from the northern Spanish region. At this time, the Goidelic Celts in Ireland were discernible linguistically by their use of the sound Q in words where British Celts would have used the sound P. Thus the Celts in Britain were known as P Celts, and the Irish as Q Celts.

1

Goidelic, therefore, was the forerunner of Modern Irish, Scots Gaelic and Manx, whilst Bretonic was the linguistic ancestor of Modern Welsh, Breton and Cornish. Whilst at first glance there seems to be very little similarity between the two forms, if we consider the split between P and Q and then examine some of the vocabulary of each language, the likeness becomes clearer: *ceann* (the Irish for head) is *penn* in Welsh; *còig* (the Scots Gaelic for five) is pemp in Breton. Also both strands reflected, until comparatively recently, the early European structure of three genders, masculine, feminine and neuter.

Thus we can see that Irish has a history stretching back to its Indo-European roots, and even today its relationship to other languages as diverse as French, Russian and Romanian is visible in certain words. The first element in the Russian placename Murmansk (a port on the Arctic Circle) is equivalent to the French *le mer*, and the Irish *an mhuir*, meaning sea. If we take the Irish for horse, *capall*, we can see that many other languages have a similar word; Romanian - *cal*, Spanish - *caballo*, French - *cheval*. These are similar due to the fact that in Indo-European the abstract concept of sea and horse, and many other words such as familial terms, remained common to the various divergent groups as they developed their own tongues.

Thus Irish stands as a modern European language related to the other European languages by its Indo-European roots and its grammatical structure, ensuring that it has an unbroken linguistic history stretching right back to its earliest formation.

2. The Early Literary Period 600-900

The history of the Irish language in its earliest periods–up to ca.1450–must rely almost exclusively on literature for its source material. Indeed factual reports on the state of the language are very scant until the establishment of bureaucracy in Tudor Ireland from around 1550 on. Until the advent of Christianity, Celtic Ireland had no written literary tradition. There was a strong oral tradition, however, with stories, tales and genealogies committed to memory. Special training had to be undertaken to learn the skills required, and those trained in the craft were considered a noble class with special privileges. With the coming of Christianity, writing was introduced for the first time. Prior to this, there was a form of script known as ogam, made up of a series of strokes and lines along the edge of standing stones. These stones can still be found today, some in England, Wales and Scotland (probably erected by Irish settlers), but most in Ireland. The inscriptions mainly consist of names in Early Celtic; due to the cumbersome system involved, it was impractical to use for anything but the shortest sentences.

The setting up of monasteries in Ireland, following the Christian church's missionary work in the country, meant that writing in the modern sense became more widespread, with monks recording significant events– such as deaths of kings and battles–in bodies of knowledge known as annals, and native tales began to be recorded for the first time. The illustrated Latin works such as *The Book of Kells* were also written in this period. For the student of linguistics, glosses (notes made in the margins of Latin manuscripts explaining Latin words and phrases, giving the Irish equivalent) are extremely useful, enabling the study of the language of the time. The best known are the Wurzburg Glosses, the Milan Glosses and the Glosses of Saint Gall.

During the Old Irish period, 600-900 A.D., the language used in the manuscripts was classical, standardised within a very rigid grammatical formula. Indeed it is quite remarkable that there is so little evidence of dialect in the writings of this period; this leads to the conclusion that writing was governed by an authority of some sort. It must be assumed that written language became further and further removed from the vernacular or spoken word, until it became an almost separate language. While ordinary people continued with the oral tradition, it was the nobility who were entertained by readings from recorded tales, thus ensuring that the written word was seen as the preserve of the educated class. This guaranteed a conservative outlook in

3

a literature so linguistically removed from that of the peasantry, although it must be remembered that the oral tradition had its own conventions, in spite of using language closer to daily speech.

Perhaps the best known non-religious text of this period is *Táin Bó Cuailgne, The Cattle Raid of Cooley.* The earliest recorded version of this tale dates from the seventh century, whilst the oldest extant manuscript dates from the tenth century. The manuscript itself makes interesting reading in that it not only records the story, but affords us a precious glimpse of the political structure of society at the time. It also stands out as a manuscript because it is three times longer than any other narrative in Early Irish tradition. It can be considered an Irish equivalent to the Greek and Roman epics such as Homer's *Iliad* or Virgil's *Aeneid.* The monks were taking a tale from the oral tradition and using it to give Ireland a heroic history comparable to that of any other European nation of the period.

The tale deals with the heroic exploits of the Ulster warriors, the Red Branch Knights. Amongst the heroes were Laoghaire, Conall Cernach, Conn Cétchathach, Fergus Mac Roich, Conchubar Mac Nessa, and probably the best known of all, Cú Chulainn. The main story concerns Medb (Maeve), and her husband Ailill, queen and king of Connaught, arguing over their possessions. They are equal in all things, except for Ailill's famous white bull. Medb arranges to borrow the brown bull of Cooley from Fachtna, an Ulster farmer, but while the Connaught men are arranging the loan, they boast that they would have taken the bull by force if their request had not been granted. On hearing this, Fachtna is furious and withdraws his offer. Medb, angry at being snubbed, raises an army consisting of her own warriors, of warriors from Leinster and Munster, and of Ulstermen in exile, led by Fergus Mac Roich; they had left King Conchubar's court in protest at Conchubar's treacherous slaying of the three sons of Uisneach, one of the foretales to the main saga.

The body of the story concerns the exploits of the warrior Cú Chulainn and the immense battle in which hundreds of heroes are slaughtered. The battle rages for days and nights until the Brown Bull impales the White Bull on its horns and tosses him so far that he is torn to pieces, which are scattered throughout Ireland. Returning to his Ulster home, the Brown Bull's heart explodes. The final tragedy unfolds when the Morrigan uses magic spirits to distract Cú Chulainn and kill him.

Throughout this narrative, we see battles of epic proportion, divine intervention, prophecy, chariot encounters–all part of the epic tradition. There is, however, an underlying misogyny in the story. It is through Medb's pride that destruction is wrought upon the island, and this could be seen as a justification for excluding women from positions of power.

The tale also serves to explain many Irish placenames. Ardee, for instance, comes from *Áth Fher Diad*, or the Ford of Ferdia, the place where the encounter between Cú Chulainn and Ferdia takes place in legend. Athlone is derived from *Áth Luain*, the Ford of the Loins, the place where the White Bull's loins land after the battle with the Brown Bull. In fact much of the narrative concerns these placename legends; this reflects *dinnseanchas* (place lore), a major genre of ancient Irish literature.

These tales remain popular today, reflecting the quality of the early literature. Among other memorable works of this period are *Iomradh Brain (The Voyage of Bran)*, from the last quarter of the seventh century, *Saltair na Rann* (an epic religious poem), and the poetry of Amairgin.

In 795 the first Viking raids took place in Ireland. The resulting tumult in the monastic world caused dramatic change in written Irish. The thread of Old Irish was broken and from it emerged Middle Irish, which, in its lack of order and system, reflected this period of upheaval. It also, however, had many positive effects.

3. The Middle Irish Period 900-1200

Partly due to the Viking invasion, the formal conservatism in the literature eventually began to decline and become superseded by language that had moved closer to the everyday speech of the people. The period between the tenth and thirteenth centuries was one of flux as far as the written word was concerned, and new words were borrowed from Norse, Welsh and Latin. The static and rigid grammar began to fall away and was replaced by forms closer to, although not immediately recognisable as, Modern Irish.

Changes derived from the grammar of the spoken language began to appear in written works for the first time, as the monasteries' archaic systems became more and more obsolete. In part this was due to the monks in the scriptoria making greater use of the spoken language. This is evident in reworkings of texts from the Old Irish period. Frequently writers made mistakes in transcription; the original language of the manuscripts had become so outdated that the writers were no longer able to handle them as confidently as before.

Many works from this period are still available to study linguistically, although this would be an arduous task for anyone but an academic. Although great breakthroughs were being made as regards the modernisation of the language, it still had far to go before it could be recognised as the language spoken and written today. This is hardly surprising when we consider that Chaucer's *Canterbury Tales* would have been written in the English in this period, and it is almost unrecognisable to the modern speaker of English.

In the later part of this era, the Fenian Cycle emerged as a body of literature. This cycle contains tales of the exploits of Fionn Mac Cumaill and his warrior (fianna) band. In some manuscripts Fionn is mentioned as the head of all the warriors during the time of Cormac Mac Airt, the ancient king of Ireland, who is thought to have ruled around 300 A.D. (although he is probably mythical). These tales had always been popular with the peasantry, as is attested by the predominance of placenames involving characters from this cycle, such as the numerous places known as *Leabaidh Diarmaid is Gráinne* (the bed of Diarmaid and Gráinne).

These tales were never recorded until this late period, although they were undoubtedly much more archaic, because those transcribing in the monasteries did not wish to encourage behaviour such as that practised by the Fianna. It was a tradition in Ireland for young landless men to band together in warrior groups and learn the trades of warfare by going out into surrounding areas and pillaging and looting in the territory of other tribes. One of their principal targets for raiding was the monastery, so it was in the monks' interest to disregard such stories.

The tales emerging at the end of this period should be set in the context of the Norman invasion, as the Normans brought with them a romantic European literary cycle. Previous to this, the monasteries had been recording works of an heroic nature, such as The Ulster Cycle and The Kings' Cycle. In this new romantic climate, the exploits of young men roaming the country and fighting became more acceptable, and were soon as popular in the monasteries and noble courts as they always had been amongst the peasantry. The tales of Fionn took their place along side tales such as *Sir Gawain and the Green Knight* and Arthurian legends.

4. The Classical Period 1200-1600

The period known as the Classical Period coincides with the Norman invasion which began in 1169. This was followed by the arrival of Henry II and the subsequent efforts to establish English rule throughout Ireland. This created a period of turmoil and conflict in the country which inevitably passed on to a clash of culture and language. By 1250 two-thirds of Ireland was under the control of the Anglo-Normans; the country, however, was almost completely Irish-speaking. From that date, the Anglo-Norman advance was pushed back, and Irish was never really under threat at this time. In fact, this is when the linguistic chaos resultant from the Middle Irish period was brought under control. Previously, differences had been springing up between the grammatical systems used by various monasteries, or even by individual monks. It was decided that the language had to be standardised, so the written language experienced less change in this classical period than in any other. There is no discernible difference between the language used at the start of this era, such as that of Giolla Bhridghde Mac Con Midhe (thirteenth century) and that found in the poetry of the sixteenth century. There was also very little to distinguish the work of a writer in Gaelic-speaking Scotland and that of a writer in Ireland.

Throughout this period many attempts were made to stamp out Irish. A document from 1285 recommends that no Irish men be appointed bishops or abbots as they "always provide their churches with Irishmen ... to maintain their language." In 1367 The Statutes of Kilkenny were a bid to stop the Anglo-Irish from becoming totally absorbed in Gaelic culture. One enactment stated, "All English men and Irish dwelling among them must use English surnames, speak English and follow English customs. If any Englishman, or Irish dwelling among the English, use Irish speech he shall be attained and his lands go to his lord till he undertake to adopt and use English. The English may not entertain or make gifts to Irish minstrels, rhymers or story-tellers." This law was patently unworkable; such was the strength of the Gaelic Order, and the *filí* (poets) continued their trade. Gofraidh Fionn Ó Dálaigh (fourteenth century) explains best how they served both Gael and Gall (English):

> *I ndán na nGall gealltair linn*
> *Gaoidhil d'ionnarba a hÉirinn,*
> *Gaill do shraoneadh tar sál soir*
> *i ndán na nGaoidheal gealltair.*

In a poem for the Gall we promise
That the Gael will be expelled from Ireland
The banishment of the Gall eastward across the sea
Is promised in a poem for the Gael.

Indeed the *cúirt filíochta* (poetic court) of the *filí* travelled from Cork to Stornaway in a Gaelic cultural world throughout this period. There are numerous examples of poets travelling to and from Scotland; this also expressed itself in terms of alliances and general communication since Irish and Scots Gaelic were mutually intelligible–basically dialects of one language. In 1315 when Edward Bruce was crowning himself King of Ireland, his advisers used the argument to the Pope that, being of one linguistic band, it was natural and satisfactory for the King of Scotland to be King of Ireland (although Bruce himself was a Norman-French speaker). As late as 1604 we have a recommendation "that ministers that can speak Irish ... be gotten out of Scotland."

Throughout the history of Irish society the *file* (poet) held an exalted position. He was considered a noble by his tribe, and was well paid for his services, being rewarded with gifts of land, cattle, horses and food. There was good reason for this: those about whom the poetry was composed had to ensure the poet was pleased with their generosity because to be satirised in verse meant a complete loss of honour. In earlier times, it was even held that to be satirised by the poet could cause sickness or deformity, thus barring the victim from holding the kingship. As an Englishman in the time of Elizabeth the First observed, "The Irishmen will not sticke to affirm that they can rime either man or beast to death."

To become a poet took many years of study, learning the tales and genealogies of the oral tradition. The poets were employed to praise their patrons and to do so they would compare them with the heroes of early Ireland, and extol the virtues and bravery of their ancestors. They had to acquire extensive knowledge, therefore, of the Irish legends and even classical Greek and Roman heroes–a difficult task since the poet did not learn from books or write down what he had learned, but had to store it all in his memory.

The various metres in which the poetry was written was even more complicated to learn. These were made up of various syllabic patterns, taking into account the number of syllables in each line and the number in the final word of the line. Furthermore, internal rhyme was used and had to be of perfect rhyming order. This rhyming was not just rhyming *coat* and *boat*; the letters

9

had to correspond to certain letter groups or the rhyme would be considered imperfect. It was also considered desirable to have the last line finish with the phrase that had opened the first line of the poem. *Séadna, séadna mór, deibhidhe* and *droighneach* are but a few examples of the various metres that had to be learnt.

It was a great honour to study at a bardic school, which was the preserve of the richer classes. It was traditional in some families for a member of each successive generation to be sent for study. These schools were very popular amongst their pupils, as can be seen when Tadhg Dall Ó hUiginn commented of his sorrow each year when he heard the call of the cuckoo, heralding the breakup of the bardic school. This is hardly surprising considering that the schools were supplied with food and drink by local nobles, and the students were well looked after by the local population.

Another art the aspiring poet had to study was that of composition. To compose a poem, the poet retired to his bed in a completely darkened room with no distractions. Lying down with a stone placed on his stomach (this came from an early pagan Celtic tradition), he would compose his lay, and the following morning would recite it in front of his professors and fellow pupils. These poems could often consist of over one hundred and fifty verses, and often the modern reader may often wish that the poet had stopped at around verse twenty; it would appear that the poet was not always taught about taste. In all it took seven years to become a fully fledged *file*, as long as it would take to become a doctor today. Then after finishing his training, the poet would set out to find a patron.

Among the more renowned Bardic poets were Geofraidh Fionn Ó Dálaigh (died 1387) in Cork, Eochadh Ó hEochadhsa in Fermanagh (1568-1617), Tadhg Óg Ó hUiginn (died 1478) in Sligo and the Taoiseach Maghnus Ó Domhnaill (1500-1563) in Donegal.

The effects of the Anglo-Norman invasion on Irish literature were twofold: first, they brought a new romantic influence to bear, as mentioned in the last chapter, and second, the monasteries were no longer the main seats of learning. In terms of the language itself, it brought in an new wave of borrowed words. The Anglo-Norman invaders themselves became great patrons of the Irish arts. Gearóid Íarla (Earl Fitzgerald d. 1398), the Lord Chief Justice from 1367, was famed for his Irish poetry. Meanwhile, the attempts to suppress Irish–referred to earlier–continued, ineffective though they were. In 1493, in Waterford we hear of a law stating "that no manere man, freman nor foraine, of the citie shall enpleade nor defende in Yrish tong agenste ony man in the court." In 1537 an "Act for the English order, habite and language" further attempted to enforce the use of English. In 1536 Henry VIII sent a letter to the town of Galway, stating, "that evry inhabitant indevor theym sefe to speke Englyshe ... and specyally that you, and evry of you, do put forth your childe to scole, to lerne to speke Englyshe."

But even in 1541 the bill to make Henry VIII king of Ireland had to be read in Irish in the Lords to ensure it was understood. This bill of 1541, however, was evidence of direct and subsequently continuing London involvement in Irish affairs, which would finally crush the Irish lords. This began firstly with the most powerful of the Anglo-Irish lords, the Kildares, who were executed in 1537. As Tudor power and influence increased, so too did reaction to it and the country became more disturbed. In 1537 Mary Tudor introduced the policy of Plantation, whereby settlers from England and Scotland were given land from dispossessed Irish, in the counties of Laois and Offaly. In 1583 the defeat of the house of Desmond was followed by another plantation in Munster. Ulster was left as the main area not under Tudor control and by 1595 it was in full scale conflict with the English monarchy. The defeat of the two main lords, O'Neill and O'Donnell at Kinsale in 1601, was a prelude to the flight of the Gaelic leaders in 1607 and the collapse of the Gaelic system. In 1609 the Plantation of Ulster was begun.

A main factor in these events was the Protestant Reformation and Henry VIII's break with Rome (1534) whereby Ireland with its Catholic leaders represented a threat to Protestant England and an ally to its league of enemies. Thus while suppression of Gaelic culture was intrinsic to Tudor efforts to establish a centralised state, attitudes to the Irish language were ambivalent. By the seventeenth century, in her reformist zeal, Elizabeth I advocated the printing of the New Testament (1603) in Irish. The change of attitude, caused by the desire to propagate the Protestant religion in the country, is something of a turning point. A Protestant catechism, compiled by John Kearney, was published in 1571, the first Irish-language book published in Ireland–although Knox's liturgy in Gaelic had been seen here in 1567. This policy of using Irish to advance the Protestant Reformation was to be used again, later in that century and in the eighteenth century.

As late as 1603 Lord Chancellor Gerrades commented that "all English, and the most part with delight, even in Dublin, speak Irish," reflecting just how strong the language was toward the closing of the classical period, the eve of the destruction of the Gaelic world. It was not to remain so for much longer. The extinction of the Irish language would serve to give permanence to the political achievement of tying Ireland to England.

This outlook was articulated by Edmund Spenser: "It hath ever been the use of the conquerors to despise the language of the conquered, and force him by all means to learn his ... the speech being Irish, the heart must needs be Irish."

5. The Fall of the Gaelic Order 1600-1800

When the Gaels were defeated at the Battle of Kinsale in 1601, the death knell was sounded for the Gaelic aristocracy. From this point on, Irish experienced an unprecedented decline. Perhaps the most crucial element to the early period of decline was the loss of Irish-speaking authorities. The Gaelic aristocracy had been destroyed and with it the kings' courts, the Brehon system of law and the bardic schools. These had all held Irish in its dominant position. The people would not naturally turn to English immediately, but the social pressures emanating from this destruction of a ruling order would gradually take their toll. Throughout this period reference is made to the strength of Irish, as in this from Francis O'Molloy in King's County (Laois) in 1676: "no language is well understood by the common people except Irish alone." This was not true, however, of Ulster, where the Plantation was at its most successful and where large tracts of the province became English-speaking. Paradoxically, however, many of the Planters came from Gàidhlig-speaking parts of Scotland. The upheavals in Ulster, however, were quite severe on a displaced Irish-speaking community.

The effects of the fall of Gaelic society were immediatly felt by the *filí*, who were losers in the new order, the poets having been left with no patronage as a result of the suppression and destruction of the noble classes. Aoghán Ó Rathaille poses the following question in his lament concerning the resultant poverty of the poets:

> *Ceist, cia cheannochadh dán ?*
> 'Question, who will buy a poem ?

Likewise, Aindrias Mac Marcais laments:

> *Gan gáire fá ghníomhradh leinbh*
> *cosc ar cheol, glas ar Ghaoidgeilg.*
> There is no laughter at children's doings
> Music is prohibited, the Irish language is in chains.

The effect upon the poets was enormous. Initially, however, some of them did not fully recognise the consequences of this dramatic change in affairs as witnessed in Iomarbha na bhFilí (1616-1624) where a protracted debate/argument developed between the poets of Ulster and Munster, focusing on parochial issues and hardly mentioning the plight of their society or their own fate. In one sense it was not surprising, for the poetry schools continued in places, and even in 1640 there is a reference to Scottish poets

13

coming over to attend such schools. Others did immediately recognise their fate and gradually they became a class of wandering minstrels, selling their trade for whatever price a much impoverished noble audience could afford. They were referred as "rakarees" (from the Irish *reacaire*-one who recites) by the authorities, who persecuted them relentlessly due to their anti-English-ness.

Much of their poetry from this period reflects a desire to return to the old Gaelic system, and a yearning to see the English driven out of the country. The wars of this century and the resultant upheaval of society were finally brought to an end by the Williamite victory in 1691 and with it the establishment of the Anglo-Irish Ascendancy. This, however, was not before the devastation inflicted during the Nine Years War of 1641-1649, after which the *file* and the people were joined in mutual misery. While the majority of people still spoke Irish, many of the remaining Irish landowners and others sought to shake off Irish, and the notion that learning English was the only way to escape from poverty became prevalent in all spheres of native society.

The poets still yearned for the return of the Irish language. They were, in one sense, the primary dispossessed by this new state of affairs, and among the poets of the 1600's were Páidrigín Haicead (1600-1654), author of "Muscail do Mhisneach, a Bhanbha" (Reawaken Your Courage, Ireland); Piarais Feiritéir (1600-1652); Cú Chonnacht Ó Dálaigh; and Dáithí Ó Bruadair (1625-1698). Ó Bruadair is interesting because, although he died at the close of the century, he was quite clearly a product of the poetry schools. Throughout this period the various metre systems were beginning to fade, with all the aforementioned poets using different metres, some old, some new. Gradually these faded although there is reference to the use of *deibhidhe* in a praise poem of 1734. Later, in the eighteenth century, a new genre began, with the old metre system now gone. Aisling (vision) poetry became more and more common, with poets such as Peadar Ó Doirnín, Aogán Ó Rathaille, Art Mac Cumhaidh, Séamus Dall Mac Cuarta and Eoghan Ruadh Ó Súilleabháin composing. These poems represent a barometer of the decline of the bardic order.

Ó Rathaille (1675 - 1728), for instance, was the initiator of the aisling genre, and in his poem "*Mac an Cheannaí*" he looks forward to the restoration of the Stuart Pretender (Charles II) and the reinstatement of the Gaelic aristocracy. The vision figure in this poem is a maiden representing Ireland, betrothed to Mac an Cheannaí, the pretender. Even though the Gaels have been routed Ó Rathaille still sees some hope, repeating the phrase "*go bhfillfidh*

Mac an Cheannaí" (until Mac an Cheannaí returns). Mac Cumhaidh was writing after the victory of William III of Orange, and his poetry is much bleaker. In *"Úirchill an Chreagáin"* (The New Creggan Graveyard) his visionary maiden invites him to accompany her away from poverty and *"Chlann Bhullaigh "* (a derogatory term for the new authorities):

> *Tá mo chroí-se ina míle céad cuid*
> *'s gan balsam féin ann a d'fhoirfeadh dom phian*
> *nuair a chluinim an Ghaeilge uilig á tréigbhéail,*
> *is caismirt Bhéarla i mbeol gach aoin.*

My heart is torn in a hundred thousand pieces
And no remedy will soothe my pain
When I hear Irish being abandoned
And the din of English in everyone's mouth.

It is in the height of the aisling period that another blow is stuck to the status of Irish with the loss, effectively, of Scotland with the defeat of the Gaelic-speaking Highland clans in the Jacobite Risings of 1715 and 1745 and the subsequent destruction of Scotland's Gaelic society.

Paradoxically, this period of darkness for the bardic order resulted in perhaps the most prodigious period of composition in centuries. Although many of the poems were not as polished as they would have been under the old order, the fact there were so many indicates the dedication of these people. Perhaps this stemmed from the realisation that their art might be snuffed out forever, and they were determined to leave their mark. As Geoffrey Keating remarked upon his compilation of *History of Ireland/Fóras Feasa ar Éireann* (1633), it would be wrong that "so honourable a land as Éire and kindreds so noble as those who had inhabited it, should pass away without mention or report of them."

The distinguished Irish scholar Osborn Bergin has indicated that the poets displayed in their work "a strong dislike of vulgarity," and their art was very much more than that of folk poet. Nevertheless, the subjugation of the Gaelic aristocracy resulted in a wider audience for their literature among the Irish-speaking peasantry. It is a tribute to the tenacity of the oral tradition that the peasants were sophisticated enough in terms of literary knowledge to appreciate their poetry; literary talent became very widespread among this class and new elements emerged. Classics from this period include *"Pairlimint Chlainn Thómais"* (1650), *"An Síoga Romhanach"* and Mícheal Ó Cléirigh's

"Annala Ríoghachta Éireann" in the seventeenth century. In the eighteenth century we have Eibhlín Dubh Ní Chonaill's *"Caoineadh Airt Uí Laoghaire"* and Brian Merriman's *"Cúirt an MheánOíche"* (1780).

6. From *An Béal Binn* to *An Béal Bocht* - The Decline 1700-1900

The shift of the language from that of the court, aristocracy and parliament to a peasant vernacular was one of the main reasons for its decline. By the nineteenth century those who had become economically successful no longer used Irish as their home language. Now, those native Irish people who were seeking to advance themselves wanted not to revive the Gaelic order, but to secure their role as British citizens politically, economically and socially. In the post-Kinsale period, the ethos changed from a political struggle into a religious struggle. Following the Williamite victory in 1691, the Penal Laws were enacted. This made clear that the social barriers in Irish society were no longer cultural but religious, with the Anglo-Irish ascendancy on top, and the Catholics and Presbyterians below.

The Irish Catholic gentry who had managed to hold onto their property began to petition for the reversal of these laws from the second half of the eighteenth century onwards. The Catholic landed and merchant middle classes accepted the political situation, and their aim was to prove their loyalty as subjects of the Crown, and to be accepted as equal to their Anglo-Irish counterparts.

Aristocrats from different backgrounds retained an interest in the Irish language, but none of them had any particular wish to see Irish returned to its earlier dominant position. Instead they developed a scholarly interest in the monastic writings and Irish antiquities. An early inspiration was the 1789 publication of Charlotte Brooke's *Reliques of Irish Poetry*, which encouraged a preoccupation that was fashionable throughout the Celtic world at this period, with MacPherson in Scotland doing something similar. In spite of the fact that a large proportion of the population still spoke Irish as their first language until the time of the Famine, it was seen by these gentry as the language of the uneducated.

The forces striving to preserve the language in this period were the poets and the priests. Although the restoration of the Stuart monarchy and the return of noble chieftains were beyond the understanding of most of the peasants, they warmed to the idea of restoring Irish culture and the Catholic religion, as expressed in the poetry. The priests wanted Irish to continue as the spoken language as it offered the best assurance, in the eighteenth century, that their flocks would be protected from the teachings of the protestant churches. In 1798 the Kerry clerics petitioned the Pope to prevent a Cork man from becoming bishop, using the fact that he knew no Irish as one of their strongest arguments.

This was only one side to the story, however. If the clergy were attempting to use Irish to isolate their flocks from ideas of the Reformation, they themselves were becoming more and more likely to use English. In 1856 Bishop Moriarty of Killarney, speaking at the funeral of his predecessor, Cornellius Egan, gave the following oration:

> In this grand old Irish tongue he loved to speak ... and a pity it is to think that in the long line of pastors who taught in that Celtic tongue, his voice should be like the last loud peal of the echo in your mountains.

Such farewell speeches concerning Irish, despite the fact it was still very much in use, served only to speed the decline in the tongue. In 1782 Catholic colleges were legalised, and the great Catholic schools in England and Europe provided a classical, English-based education for those middle-class Irish Catholics who could aspire to it. This Anglicising trend was also adopted at Maynooth, which was founded in 1795. This trend gave weight to the perception that Irish was the preserve of the poor and illiterate. The hedge schools springing up in the eighteenth century served the peasantry's desire to have their children taught English, and those active in the agrarian societies such as the Whiteboys had to have enough English to write out their threats to the landlords.

At this period we finally begin to get an idea of the number of Irish speakers in the country. One of the earliest approximations deals with 1731 and estimates that two-thirds of the country were using Irish as their daily speech; this, however, was written in 1851. It is not until 1799 that we get an estimate from Whitley Stokes who gives a total of 2.4 million out of 4.75 million based on his parish survey. This study is interesting as it shows the areas of strength and weakness for Irish. In it he lists Antrim, Down, Fermanagh and Armagh as Ulster counties where the language is weak, and Wicklow, Wexford, Queens County (Offaly), Kings County (Laois), Kildare and Dublin as weak areas in Leinster. Munster and Connacht were still substantially Irish-speaking.

Other statistical, parochial and personal surveys for the period up to about 1830 give the following picture: that in Kilkenny parishes bordering on Carlow, many could speak English but used Irish among themselves; that in Longford English was universally known but not used among the Irish themselves; and that in districts of Louth, English was gaining ground. In Antrim Irish was used in the mountainous parts, as was the case also in Armagh and Derry. Other surveys said that English was making progress in parts of Clare, Limerick, East Tipparary, Leitrim and Roscommon.

It is at this time that the next blow was struck to Irish in the form of the National School system set up in 1831. The practice of Irish-speaking parents having their children punished at school for not speaking English was widespread, obviously a spur to young people to leave Irish behind them. The National School system of educating only through English is blamed for the decline in the language; indeed Pádraig Mac Piarais (Patrick Pearse) called it "The Murder Machine." The authorities obviously wanted Irish children to be brought up as loyal subjects, and ridding the country of Irish speakers was seen as helpful, although by this stage the process was well under way.

The nineteenth century was one of rapid decline for the Irish language and the final and most severe blow was struck by the Great Famine of 1845-1848, which killed over a million people and caused the emigration of a further million and a half, primarily in the most Irish-speaking areas of the west of Ireland. Those who were emigrating learned English as a necessity to help them find employment; those who remained learned English in an effort to ensure economic security. This attitude still prevailed long after the Famine. When Pádraig Mac Piarais visited Rosmuc over fifty years later, he tried to give a speech concerning the need to cherish the native language. The meeting was brought to an early conclusion when a voice shouted from the floor, "*Is beag an mhaith í nuair a ghabhann tú thar an Teach Dóite*" (It is little use when you go past the burnt house).

Immediately after the Famine, in 1851, we get the first Census return, which gives a figure of a million and a half, or about 20% of the population, speaking Irish. It was the majority language in counties Clare (59.8), Kerry (61.5%), Cork (52.5%), Waterford (62.6%), Galway (61.4%) and Mayo (65.6%) and was substantially spoken in counties Donegal, Sligo, Limerick, and Roscommon. These figures are dubious because of suspicions in the population as to why the government would be asking about Irish, and indeed it is generally accepted that many returned themselves as ignorant of Irish because of their fears. This also hides the grinding poverty of the majority of Irish speakers, many of whom who would in subsequent years emigrate in the mass exodus that continued following the Famine years.

Ireland itself, apart from the Famine, was in the throes of political agitation in a century that saw Catholic Emancipation (1829), the Repeal Movement (1830's and 1840's), Young Ireland (1840's), the Fenians (1850's and 1860's) the Land League and Home Rule movements (1870's onward), and the growing involvement of the people in popular politics led to increased Anglicisation as the demand for information grew. In the earlier period of the agrarian secret societies, most of the Irish peasantry were ignorant of national politics. Although they suffered greatly in the United Irishmen's rebellion of 1798, the ideal of a secular libertarian republic was totally unknown to them. Indeed the rising in Wexford, caused more by grievance and fear than by the grand ideals of the United Irishmen, shows more accurately the understanding of the peasantry, and saw members of the Cork Militia plead for their lives in a language totally unintelligible to the Wexford peasantry: Irish!

This earlier political isolation helped ensure the survival of the language in its strongholds. The political mass movements of the nineteenth century, which had begun with ideas of the United Irishmen, soon changed this. Although this group did endeavour to forward some idea of the place of the language in society and even succeeded in producing the first ever journal in Irish, *Bolg an Tsolair* (1795), subsequent political movements ignored Irish almost completely. Songs celebrating the 1798 Rebellion were composed, but they were along the lines of "The Croppy Boy" and "The Shan Van Vocht." The primary culprit in Anglicising mass-movement politics was Daniel O'Connell, who led both the Emancipation and Repeal Movements up to the 1840's. Although a fluent Irish speaker, he refused to use the language at his Monster Meetings and all propaganda was in English. This trend continued throughout the century, with such notable exceptions as Thomas Davis of the Young Ireland movement (1840's) and the Fenian O'Donovan Rossa (1860's onward). The speeches from the dock of men like John Mitchel and the mass meetings were all in English. The growing emigrant community received their propaganda in English, and both those at home and abroad adopted William Drennan's sentimental ideas of the "Emerald Isle" and the harp and shamrock as symbols of national expression–rather than the language itself.

By 1891, therefore, two years before *Conradh na Gaeilge* (The Gaelic League) was formed to save the language, we can see the full effect of National Schools, emigration and a negative attitude to Irish shown to an increasingly aware people. The census results for that year show Irish as the majority language in Galway (58.5%) and Mayo (50.4%). Of the other counties mentioned for 1851 we have the following figures: Clare (37.7%), Kerry (41.4%), Cork (31.0%) and Waterford (46.9%). In Sligo (21.8%), Roscommon (10.4%) and Limerick (13.1%), it had all but died out. Only Donegal showed progress (33.4%). Overall, this is a substantial decrease for a period of only forty years. By this stage the language was in serious difficulties and even in the field of literature we can see a decline in both quantity and quality. A number of folk poets, such as Art Mac Bonaid in south Armagh, still kept the poetic heritage alive and others such as Amhlaoibh Ó Súilleabháin introduced other elements with his *Cinnlae Amhlaoibh Ó Shúilleabháin* in 1826-1836. Generally, however, the language in all aspects was in serious decline.

7. The Revival Movement 1800-1921

In the eighteenth up to the middle of the nineteenth century, although the aristocracy and clergy were giving eulogies upon the death of the Irish tongue, there was little danger of it passing away as a vernacular for most of the population. Before the Famine, population growth meant that there were more Irish speakers in the country than there had been at any other time in its history. However, we have seen that education and politicisation through English as well as the desire for economic betterment and emigration were already contributing to its rapid decline. Then the tragedy of the Famine swept away a vast number of the remaining Irish speakers.

The pre-famine Irish revival movements were scholarly in character, and conservative and aristocratic in outlook. Organisations such as The Gaelic Society of Dublin (founded 1807), the Iberno-Celtic Society (1818) and the Irish Archaeological Society (1840) had little or no interest in contemporary Irish writing. They saw the Irish peasantry as shrewd, but with little real intellectual worth. These movements concentrated on the study of manuscripts and antiquities.

It was in Ulster that Presbyterians came to the fore in their defence of the language. One early pioneer was Rev. William Neilson, who published his *Introduction to the Irish Language* in 1808. Perhaps the earliest society to take an interest in the contemporary language was the *Cuideacht Gaoidheilge Uladh* (Ulster Gaelic Society), founded in 1830 by people like Robert McAdam, Samuel Bryce and Dr. MacDonnell. MacAdam, who had helped open an Irish school at Ballynascreen in 1828 was to the fore in the Society's 1835 Irish grammar for use in Royal Belfast Acadamy and their 1837 publication *Bolg a T-Solair*. Other publications followed, schools were set up and lobbying continued. Like many early societies, however, the Ulster Gaelic Society ceased effective functioning by 1843 although those involved continued their work.

The real origins of the revival lie in the writings of Thomas Davis. He was almost a lone voice advocating the cultivation of Irish as a living and vibrant tongue. Whilst other scholars tended to ignore the contemporary vernacular, Davis was of the opinion that as a language it should be cherished and esteemed. In many respects his ideas were those that had such a profound influence upon the later thinking of the Gaelic League. He foreshadowed Pádraig Mac Piarais' bilingual programme when he declared:

Simply requiring the teachers of the National Schools in these Irish speaking districts to know Irish, and supplying them with Irish translations of the school books would guard the language, where it now exists, and prevent it from being swept away by the English tongue.

Others who attempted to stem the growing tide of English included Philip Barron, who set up an Irish College in Bonmahon, Co. Waterford, in 1835, and Richard D'Alton who produced the publication *An Fíor-Éireannach* in Tipperary in 1862. Both advocated the revival of the language as the national tongue, planning societies in towns and villages throughout the country. Both, however, were unsuccessful due to lack of funding and support.

In 1878 Archbishop John MacHale of Tuam succeeded in having "Celtic" recognised as a subject in Intermediate schools. He was the patron of The Society for the Preservation of the Irish Language. Amongst the prominent members of this society were Douglas Hyde, David Comyn and Michael Cusack. From this sprang a new movement, The Gaelic Union, which was dedicated to publishing books in Irish, and to reprinting Irish texts for use in Intermediate schools. They set up *The Gaelic Journal* in 1882, marking a turning point in the revival movement. It enabled enthusiasts to develop their ideas and literary skills in modern Irish.

In 1893 the most influential of the revival bodies was set up - The Gaelic League (Conradh na Gaeilge). Its foundation marked the beginning of the reaction against Anglicisation, which developed in many aspects of Irish society in the run up to the Easter Rising. From the outset it was exclusively concerned with the revival of Irish as the spoken vernacular of the entire nation and the creation of a new literature. Although it grew slowly at first, it soon gained in size. In this it was helped by the publication of Father O'Growney's *Simple Lessons in Irish*, which made Irish accessible to the general public, and by the appointment of *timirí* (organisers) to work locally and provincially. In 1901 there were 120 branches throughout the country; by 1904 this had increased to 593.

To solve the problem of a lack of teachers qualified to teach through Irish, *Coláiste na Mumhan* was set up in Ballingeary, running summer schools for teachers of the language. Soon other Colleges were set up in Gaeltacht (Irish-speaking) regions. To make classes more accessible, the lessons were run in conjunction with dancing and music lessons. *Feiseanna* were run locally and annually a nationwide *Oireachtas* (festival of culture) was held.

Prizes were presented to the most proficient in the language in all age groups.

The League took over the running of *The Gaelic Journal* in 1894, using it to promote a new body of Irish literature. Other publications soon followed -*Fáinne an Lae* and An *Claidheamh Soluis* - and soon these journals were providing a forum for literature, discussion and debate on all aspects of the language revival. The English language was used to stress the importance of "Irish Ireland," and many pamphlets on this topic were published. These ensured that those with no Irish could become interested, and numbers increased accordingly.

Thanks to the efforts of Douglas Hyde, the position of Irish in the Intermediate schools was greatly improved by 1900. In 1904 the League secured acceptance of bilingual education in primary schools in Irish-speaking regions. Perhaps their hardest battle and their greatest triumph was to secure Irish as an essential subject for the matriculation in the National University.

Although the League went from strength to strength, founding a new literature and increasing people's ability to read and converse in the native language, it had many failures, mainly for two reasons: Irish still was stigmatised as the language of the illiterate and the ill-educated, and no body could restore the language without large-scale government backing.

This Irish language revival must be set against the background of a national revival running through all spheres of Irish life, for which the Gaelic League was both a catalyst and a beneficiary. Michael Cusack's Gaelic Athletic Association in 1884, the encouragement of Irish dancing and singing, and the growing aggression of nationalist political movements such as Arthur Griffith's Sinn Féin (1907) were all influential as national developments leading up to the Easter Rising of 1916 and the subsequent War of Independence (1919-1921), from which the Irish Free State emerged. It is not surprising that the Gaelic League was suppressed by the British government in 1919. To most of the people leading the campaign for independence, the two struggles - language and independence - were inextricably bound together. As Michael Collins stated,

> We only succeeded after we had begun to get back our Irish ways; after we had made a serious effort to speak our language; after we had striven to govern ourselves. .... The biggest task will be the restoration of the language.

8.The Emerging State and the Irish Language 1921-1994

It would be false to say that the acheivements of the Gaelic League were a panacea to the problems affecting the language. In the nineteenth century the formal education system ignored the existence of Irish, and in general sought "to encourage the cultivation of the English language, and to make English the language of the schools." The League, and the new state were guided by Pádraig Mac Piarais' conviction as laid out in an editorial of *An Claidheamh Soluis:*

> Had the education of the country been sane and national for the last hundred years, there would never have been a necessity for the language movement; when it is thoroughly sane and national again in all its branches, the necessity for the language movement will have ceased.

In the move towards independence, the language question had become more and more of a priority. The Irish language in education was now a central policy matter in the new independent parliament (Dáil Éireann) established in 1919. Indeed most of the first session of the new Dáil was conducted in Irish. The prominence of the Gaelic League in formulating the policy was guaranteed by the appointment of the League's president, Seán Ó Ceallaigh, as Minister for Irish in the first Dáil cabinet; he later became Minister of Education. The prominence of the issue was ensured by the participation in the new political structures of such figures as Michael Collins, Eoin Mac Neill, Richard Mulcahy, Cathal Brugha, Ernest Blythe, Éamon de Valera, Seán Ó Ceallaigh and Seán T. Ó Ceallaigh, who were all members of the Gaelic League.

To ensure cultivation of the language, in the Gaeltacht Irish would be the language of instruction in the schools, a bilingual programme would be initiated in those areas that were bilingual, and in English-speaking areas, Irish would be taught for an hour each day by a competent teacher. In all the schools, Irish was to be the language of administration.

The Provisional Government, and the later Free State Government entrusted the Ministry of Education with the "Gaelicising of Ireland." The initial period up until the end of the 1940's saw an enthusiasm for the revival with all state bodies named in Irish only, political parties named in the Irish language, a good deal of Irish-language broadcasting by the state's new radio station Radió Éireann and other projects such as placing Irish-speaking communities on good land outside the Gaeltacht with a view to Gaelicising surrounding English-speaking areas and eventually joining up with the expanding Gaeltacht. Of the few that were attempted before this policy was abandoned, the Meath Gaeltacht still survives and flourishes in Ráth Cairn. A Gaeltacht Commission was set up to improve the everyday life of the people of these poor and rugged areas as well as giving financial inducements to families who retained Irish as their language. In spite of these measures, however, the Gaeltacht did not expand. County Clare is a case in point: In 1891 there were 46,878 (37.7%) Irish speakers. In 1936, in the Gaeltacht areas (not, therefore, the full county), there were 17,124 and by 1946 this was down to 11,978.

Today Clare is not a Gaeltacht region. The decades following World War Two/The Emergency saw a gradual decrease in either government interest or hope of restoring the language, and by the 1960's it was faced by pressure groups such as Muintir na Gaeltachta, Amárach and Misneach, all set up from within the Gaeltacht and who eventually compelled government to set up Raidió na Gaeltachta in 1967. Other campaigns have followed as the state, with a number of exceptions, increasingly moves to integrate itself with Europe and considers Irish both an obstacle and a financial burden. The responsibilities as laid out in *Bunreacht na hÉireann* (The Irish Constitution of 1937), Article 8, Section 1, are forgotten: "*Os í an Ghaeilge an teanga naisiúnta is í an phríomhtheanga oifigiúil í*" (The Irish language as the national language is the first official language).

Increasingly the state has provided material in English only, new state bodies have been named in English only and political parties from 1970 on, have had English as their primary name. It was only after serious pressure from grassroots organisations that the government finally agreed to set up Telefís na Gaeilge (all Irish television channel) in 1994, twelve years after the setting up of Sianel 4 Cymru (Welsh language broadcasting channel) in Wales. Sianel 4 Cymru broadcast its first programme on November 1, 1982. Telefís na Gaeilge has not yet finalised a launch date.

The State's lack of interest contrasts with a burgeoning populist revival in the South in recent decades. For example, the Gaelscoileanna - a network of Irish-medium schools outside the Gaeltacht ranging from pre-schools to secondary schools - has grown from 11 in 1971 to over 80 in 1993; all these were set up without state involvement, though usually getting state funding in due course. New independent groups are starting to agitate or make their own agenda such as Cumhacht in Conamara and Gael-Taca in Cork and community initiatives are developing both in Gaeltacht areas and in the cities. Independent publishers are also developing: Coiscéim in Dublin and Cló Iar-Chonnachta.

Literature, too, has blossomed in this period. Initially, in the period after independence much Irish literature, with exceptions such as Pádraic Ó Conaire, Liam Ó Flaithearta and Seosamh Mac Grianna, had a Gaeltacht setting and a feel for the romantic or the true-Gael. This image took a knock with the publication of *An Béal Bocht* by Myles na gCopaleen in 1941 which shook Irish literature into a new era, mirroring the social development of the country. Subsequent work came from Seán Ó Ríordáin, Máirtín Ó Díreáin in the fields of poetry and the short story and novel was developed by Máirtín Ó Cadhain, Eoghan Ó Tuairisc and Domhnall Mac Amhlaidh. Drama, meanwhile, was being catered for by playwrights of the stature of Breandán Ó Beacháin. Today poets such as Nuala Ní Dhomhnaill, Gabriel Rosenstock, Cathal Ó Searcaigh, writers such as Séamas Mac Annaidh and Pádraig Standún, and playwrights such as Antoine Ó Flatharta have added to this literary renaissance.

At present then, Irish is catered for by the State through a network of organisations like Bord na Gaeilge, publishing ventures like An Gúm and the weekly *Anois*; an unimaginative language policy in schools and a somewhat minimalist approach from state broadcasting authorites. However, it is in the more independent groups such as Gaelscoileanna, Cumhacht and Dublin's Raidió na Life that the language is genuinely making advances. Another such innovative project was launched in 1962. Called Glór na nGael, it is a national competition awarding prizes to the areas that do the most to promote Irish in the community. Starting with 45 committiees in 1962, by 1992 it had 165 communities working for the Irish language. In many cases it has been independent grassroots groups that have spurred change such as the setting up of Raidió na Gaeltachta, the forthcoming Telefís na Gaeilge, improvement in the Gaeltacht and literary initiatives such as the monthly magazine *Comhar*.

9. The Irish Language in the North 1921-1994

In the North, the foundation of the new state saw Irish being viewed by the authorities as a foreign language of no relevance. This, in spite of the fact that in 1851 and 1891 respectively the figures for Irish speakers in the six counties that would come under its jurisdiction were as follows: Antrim 3,033 (1.2%) and 885 (0.4%): Armagh 13,736 (7.0%) and 3,486 (2.4%) Derry 5,406 (2.8%) and 2,723 (1.8%) Down 1,153 (0.4%) and 590 (0.3%) Fermanagh 2,704 (2.3%) and 561 (0.8%) and Tyrone 12,892 (5.0%) and 6,687 (3.9%). Indeed on the setting up of the Northern Irish state in 1921, there were Gaeltacht regions in Antrim, Armagh, Tyrone and Derry.

A dispute over education eventually saw the setting up of two systems: state education, which provided mainly for Protestants, and maintained education, which catered mainly for Catholics, thus ensuring that Irish would not be taught at all in state schools, as there was no demand for it.

The Stormont parliament displayed antipathy at best, and outright hostility at worst, toward the language. This outlook led to a number of measures to outlaw the language, such as the Public Health and Local Government Miscellaneous Provisions of 1949, effectivly forbidding the erection of streetnames in Irish.

The Northern language movement could not adequately compete with its Southern counterparts. Irish was not heard on radio or later on television. It was not used politically, nor was it encouraged or recognised by the authorities. Developments for the period 1921 to 1970 include the setting up of the Ardscoil in Divis; the foundation of *An tUltach* magazine (1926), still the longest running Irish periodical in existence; and the building of Cumann Chluain Ard in Belfast, an Irish language club and society. It culminated in the Shaw's Road housing scheme in the late sixties when a number of language activists set up their own "mini-Gaeltacht" in Belfast.

Having established this "mini- Gaeltacht," they set up their own school (Bunscoil Pobail Feirste) in 1971 to teach their children through Irish. This, the first Irish-medium school in the North, only admitted children of parents whodid not speak Irish in 1978. The school developed slowly and, since the education authorities refused to recognise it, it was funded solely through voluntary effort.

Toward the end of the 1980's, the work of earlier pioneers began to be organised through the Irish club Cumann Chluain Ard. This concurred with a greater interest in the Irish language and culture, in part influenced by the Hunger Strikes of 1981, with one of the Hunger Strikers, in particular, Bobby Sands, highlighting the language through his writings. Spurred by this intensified climate developments proceeded apace. Irish-language classes took off, and more and more children were sent to the Bunscoil. That year saw the publication in Belfast of a weekly newspaper in Irish, *Preas an Phobail*.

In 1982 the first Irish-language pre-school was set up in the Short Strand; by 1984 there were four. This same year saw a number of other developments: *Lá*, the first daily newspaper in Irish (or any Celtic language) ever, was published in Belfast, and that summer the Bunscoil was officially recognised by the Education Department and grant aided. Bilingual signs were being erected in defiance of the law and shops and businesses were using Irish signs. Also in 1984 Bunscoil Bhaile Stíle opened in Derry. By 1987 the Belfast Bunscoil had four hundred pupils and was unable to take any more. In 1987 Gaelscoil na bhFál, Belfast's second Irish-language primary school, was set up. In that year there were 7 pre-schools.

One of the main dynamos behind this movement was the West Belfast Committee of Glór na nGael, set up in 1982. which had also successfully fought the government's proposals to downgrade Irish in the English-speaking education system in 1988. Indeed such was their success that in 1987 and again in 1991 Belfast succeeded in taking the top prizes in the national Glór na nGael competition for the area doing most to promote Irish. In 1993 Derry took the prize.

In 1990, however, Belfast Glór na nGael lost a grant for workers from the government due to unfounded and unproven allegations of links with paramilitaries. A huge public outcry followed and a campaign started, lasting two years and ending in a court case before the government finally restored the funding. Meanwhile, the language had continued to develop. In 1990, backed by the government, Iontaobhas Ultach was set up to look at ways of funding Irish-language projects. This was a remarkable milestone, being the first direct government involvement in Irish-language promotion in the North. In 1991 the census, for the first time since 1911, asked about the number of Irish speakers. The results showed 142,000 able to speak the language (29,000 in Belfast alone). 1991 also saw a major step in the development of Irish language education with the opening of Meánscoil Feirste (secondary school) in Belfast with 9 pupils; by 1994 it had over 70 pupils. In 1992 Gaelscoil na bhFál got maintained status from the Department of Education. By then there were also

Irish-speaking primary schools in Newry and Maghera, a pre-school in Armagh, and some district councils such as Newry and Mourne, Fermanagh, Derry and Strabane had started using Irish on signposts and in publications. In 1993 a third Bunscoil opened in Belfast in Whiterock and by September 1994 there was a secondary school in Derry; a fourth primary school opened in Ardoyne in Belfast and Tyrone opened its first pre-school in Strabane. Plans are well advanced for other pre-schools and bunscoileanna in places such as Downpatrick, Carrickmore and Dungannon.

In the field of media, *Lá*, the Irish-language daily, decided to publish on a weekly basis from 1993, giving the paper an even higher standard of quality. English-language newspapers and magazines have, however, increasingly added Irish to their pages with the *Irish News* and *Fortnight* regularly featuring Irish. BBC Radio Ulster started broadcasting programmes in Irish in 1982. Today they have a wide and varied range of programmes throughout the week, and BBC TV have made a number of documentaries in Irish. Eventually, in 1993, Ulster Television produced a series of children's programmes in Irish (*Tomás an Traein*, Thomas the Tank Engine).

In a society where dispute over national and cultural identity has led to violent conflict, the Irish language movement has had reasonable success in maintaining a linguistic basis to the revival, trying to leave the way open for people of all opinions to learn the language. Developments in this field include a range of classes, mini-colleges and lectures in "neutral" venues and others in what are loyalist areas of Belfast. This sphere is just beginning to develop, but has led many who might have been wary of the language movement to now view it in a positive, or at least non-reactive, light.

Still there are a number of legal barriers. In 1991 the Secretary of State Peter Brooke, while stating that government policy was not going in the direction of promoting a bilingual society, said that the act preventing the use of Irish street names would be removed. This, however, does not mean that Irish is given a legal status. That will happen only when it is given full parity with English in the mechanisms of the state: the right to have official documents in Irish, to use Irish in the courts, to have official bilingual placenames where they are wanted, by local people and equally importantly, to have the active promotion of the language - not the reactive policy of the preceding years.

Meanwhile, the Irish-speaking community continues to move apace, with community initiatives far outstripping government response. In 1991

Cultúrlann McAdam Ó Fiaich was opened as a cultural centre in West Belfast. It hosts a cafe, bookshop, the office of *Lá*, a theatre used by Aisteoirí Aon Dráma, the office of Taca, an independent lottery used to raise funds for the language and Raidió Fáilte, a not-yet-legal radio station which broadcasts throughout Belfast. In May of 1994 a conference was held to investigate future employment trends and potentials for the Irish-speaking community, following a report by Glór na nGael showing that over 220 people were earning a living in Belfast while working through the Irish language. Outside Belfast, Newry and Mourne District Council has an Irish-language officer, and in Derry plans are afoot to open their own Cultúrlann. In the countryside many local committees are now exploring the possibilities of setting up both pre-schools and primary schools. Such now is the strength of the Northern revival that the South often finds itself looking North for inspiration. Both parts of the country, however, are experiencing a language renaissance, this time built on the solid foundations of community involvement and education through the Irish language.

Map 1.......... Gaelic World c.1500

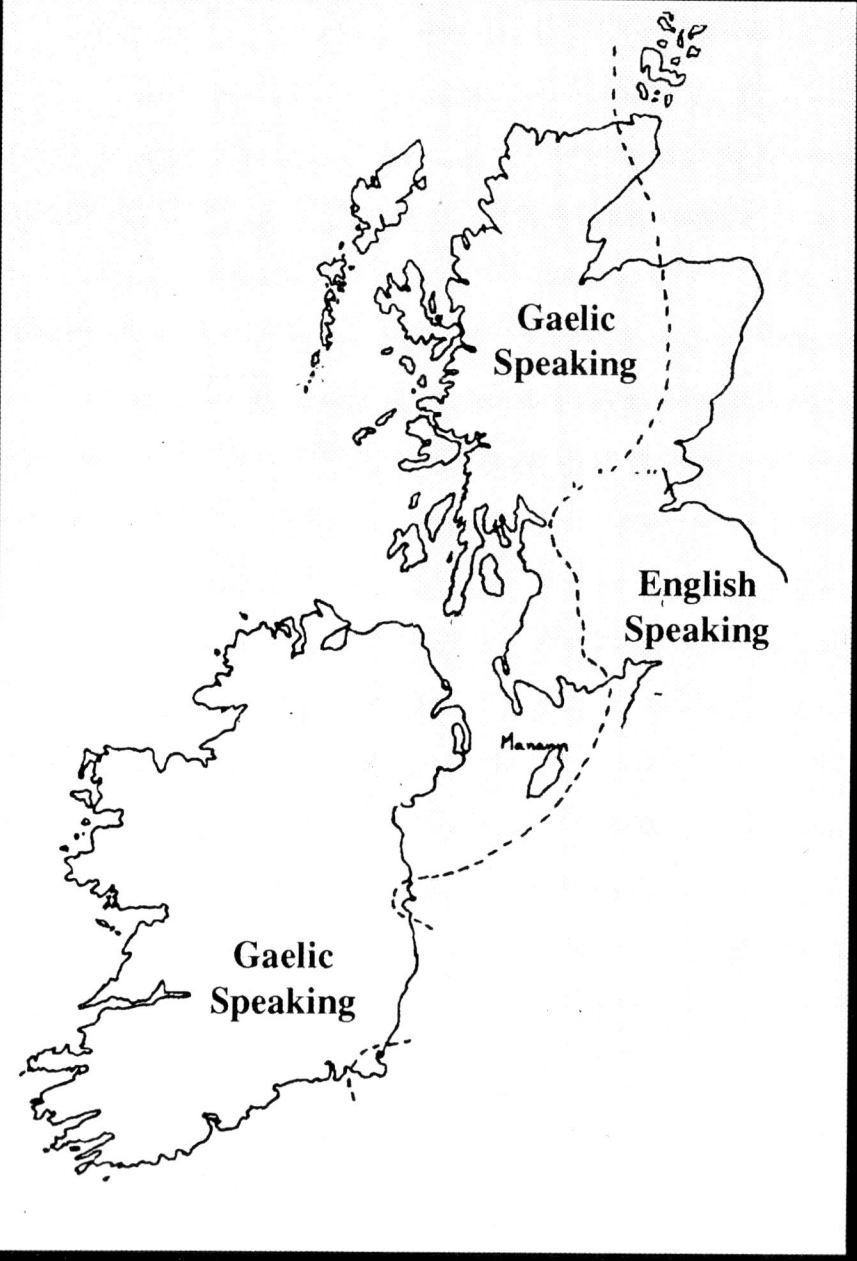

Gaelic
Speaking

English
Speaking

Manann

Gaelic
Speaking

Map 2 State of Irish 1851

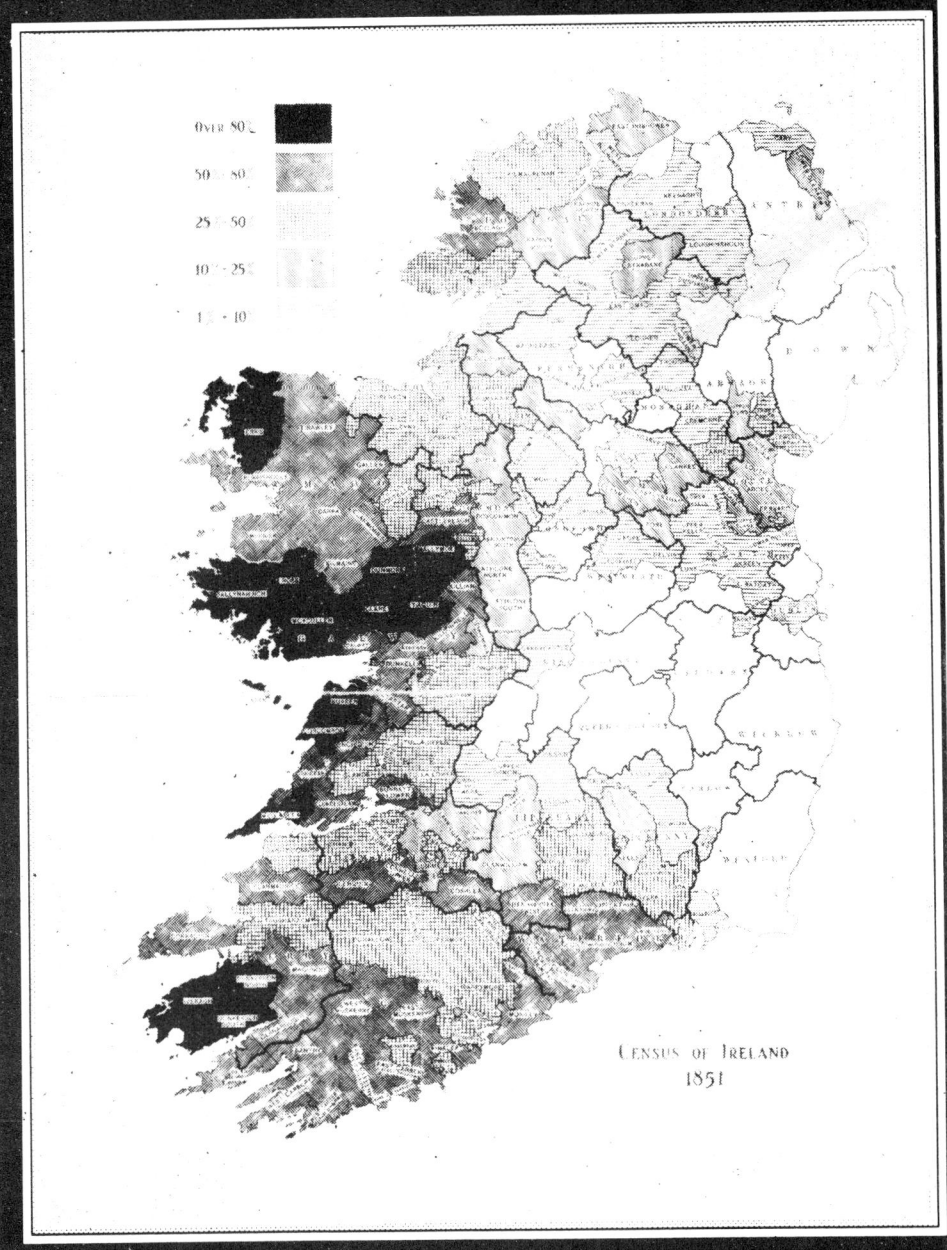

CENSUS OF IRELAND
1851

Map 3. Position of Irish Today

a) Nos refer to Gaelscoileanna outside Gaeltacht
b) Shaded areas is Gaeltacht proper
c) Other initiatives regarding language

LÁ
Cultúrlann
Mc Adam Ó Fiaich

Raidió na Life
Comhar
Bord na Gaeilge

Raidió
na
Gaeltachta

Gael -Taca

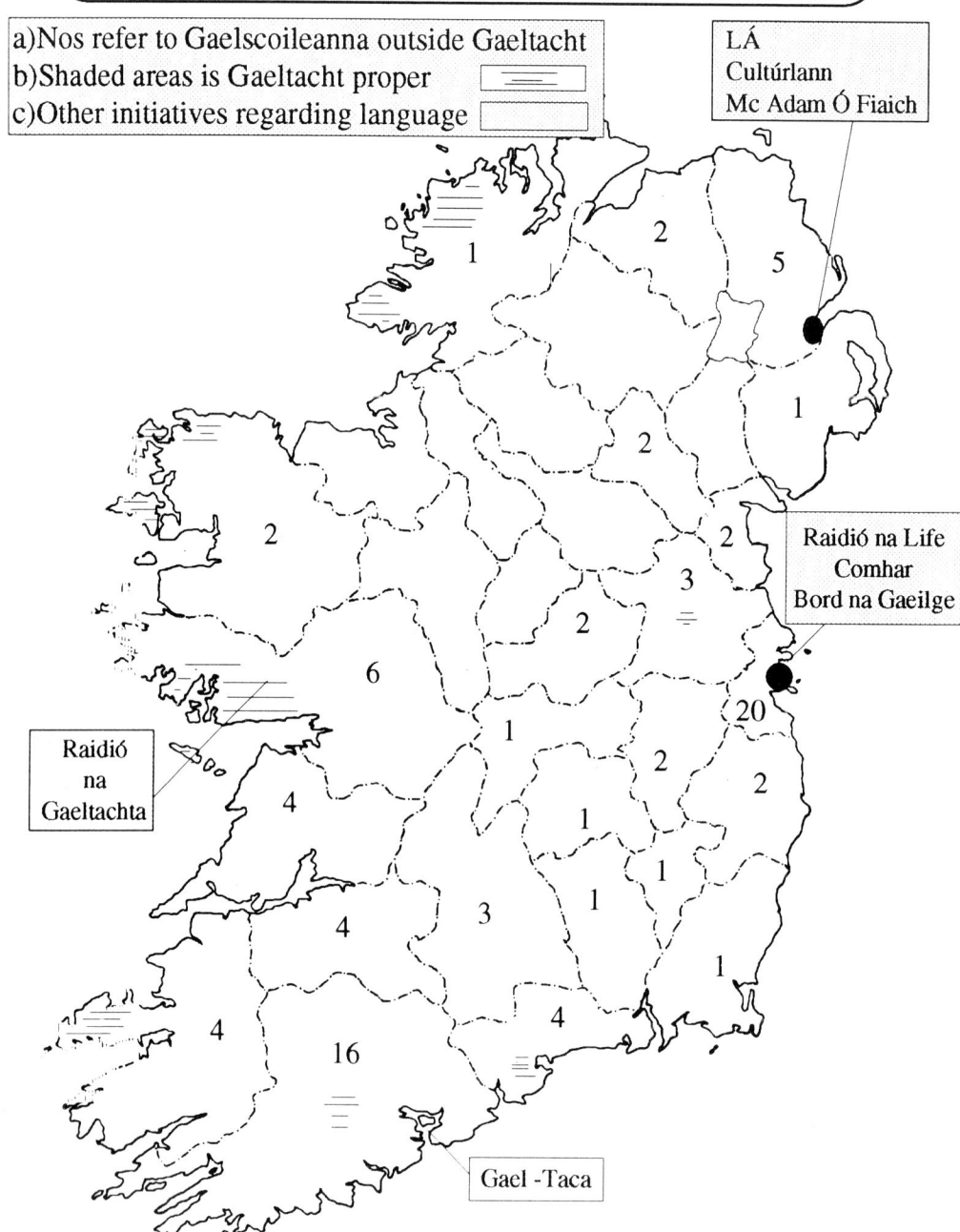

34

References

1 *Traidisiúin Liteartha na nGael.* J.C. Caerwen Williams agus Máirín Ní Mhuiríosa. An Clóchomhar. 1985

2 *Irish Dialects and Irish Speaking Districts* Brian Ó Cuív. Dublin Institute for Advanced Studies. 1951

3 *Stair Soisialta and Cultúrtha na Gaeilge* Máirtín Ó Murchú. Leabhrán Ollscoile.

4 *Hidden Ulster.* Pádraig Ó Snodaigh. Clódhanna Teo.1977

5 *The History of the Celtic People.* Henry Hubert.

6 *A View of the Irish Language.* Ed. Brian Ó Cuív. Stationary Office. 1969

Further Reading

1 *The Irish Language.* David Greene. Mercier Press. 1972

2 *Early Irish Literature.* Myles Dillon. University of Chicago Press. 1948

3 *The Pleasures of Gaelic Literature.* Editor John Jordan. Mercier Press. 1980

4 *Our Own Language.* Gabrielle Maguire. Multilingual Matters. 1990

5 *Stair na Gaeilge.* Various editors. Má Nuad. 1995

Glór na nGael Bhéal Feirste Thiar
West Belfast Glór na nGael

Glór na nGael is a national competition to identify the area doing the most to promote the Irish language. The West Belfast committee of Glór na nGael was set up in 1982. Today its main remits of work are in pre-school and adult education, social and economic policy for Irish speakers and the rights of Irish language speakers. The committee also seeks to help fledging projects further their initiatives through resources and support and produces a monthly bi-lingual magazine called An Fhearsaid.

Details on West Belfast Glór na nGael's activities including classes, publications and policy can be got from;

145 Bóthar na bhFál, Béal Feirste 12 6AF *Phone* **(01232) 232608**